THE CHINESE ART OF PLACEMENT

Stanley Rutherford

BROADWAY PLAY PUBLISHING INC
New York
www.broadwayplaypublishing.com
info@broadwayplaypublishing.com

THE CHINESE ART OF PLACEMENT
© Copyright 1999 Stanley Rutherford

All rights reserved. This work is fully protected under the copyright laws of the United States of America. No part of this publication may be photocopied, reproduced, stored in a retrieval system, or transmitted, in any form or by any means, electronic, mechanical, recording, or otherwise, without the prior permission of the publisher. Additional copies of this play are available from the publisher.

Written permission is required for live performance of any sort. This includes readings, cuttings, scenes, and excerpts. For amateur and stock performances, please contact Broadway Play Publishing Inc. For all other rights please contact the author c/o B P P I.

First published by B P P I in September 1999 in *Plays From Woolly Mammoth*

First edition: August 2020
I S B N: 978-0-88145-889-3

Book design: Marie Donovan
Page make-up: Adobe InDesign
Typeface: Palatino

THE CHINESE ART OF PLACEMENT was originally presented at the Phoenix Theater in San Francisco in February 1998, produced by Linda Ayres-Frederick. The cast and creative contributor were:

SPARKY LITMAN .... John Robb
Director .... Glynis Rigsby

THE CHINESE ART OF PLACEMENT had its East Coast premiere at Woolly Mammoth on 7 June 1999. The cast and creative contributors were:

SPARKY LITMAN .... Howard Shalwitz
Director .... Lee Mikeska Gardner
Set design .... Robin Stapley
Lighting design .... Jay Herzog
Sound design .... Hana Sellers
Stage manager .... Stephanie Nagle

CHARACTER & SETTING

Sparky Litman

Sparky Litman's *home*
Time: The present

(The stage is bare except for an old chair downstage right. At lights up, SPARKY LITMAN, *a man in his late forties, stands studying the position of the chair. He crosses and moves the chair slightly upstage, stands back, studies its position, moves it slightly again, stands back and studies the whole space.)*

SPARKY: I used to be a poet.

(He studies the placement of the chair again, then moves it slightly downstage, then walks away from it, turns back, and studies it for a moment.)

But the time came when I stopped being a poet, because I became normal, and after I became normal I didn't have anything to write poetry about anymore. And so now I have time to do other things.

(Beat, as he adjusts the position of the chair.)

And I for one am extremely relieved that I'm not writing poetry anymore, and there are a lot of other people who are extremely relieved that I'm not writing poetry anymore, because it was bitter poetry…angry, heart-wrenching poetry that caused a lot of people a lot of pain, and now that I'm not writing poetry anymore they don't have to suffer and neither do I.

(He crosses and moves the chair back to where it was at the start, stands back and studies it.)

It's important where you place the chair…and they don't tell ya' about that in school like a lot of other important things that they don't tell ya' about in school, and where you place the chair influences everything important like health, happiness, wealth and longevity, and I've been enjoying extremely good health, robust good health, and aside from the diet and the occasional exercise and the improved mental attitude now that I'm not writing poetry any more, I feel that a lot of it has to do with the fact that now *I know* that *where* you place the chair is important, and I've decided to place the chair in the position of the benefactors. And I've been spending a lot of time sitting here in the chair in the position of the benefactors, thinking about the benefactors, thinking about how if maybe they'd left me a little money, ya' know what I mean, everything'd be a whole lot different….

(Beat)

I used to keep the chair up here

(He indicates.)

in the position of the children…which was stupid, and I'll admit that, because I don't have any children, and to place the chair in the position of the children when you don't have any children or want to have any children is like putting the chair on the north side of the tree when you want to be in the sun, okay. And if maybe you *wanted* to have children, and let me just say right now that I don't want to have children, I've never wanted to have children, and I've never understood people who *do* want to have children, and okay, you know what I mean, if you *wanted* to have children, then sure, okay, that's it, you *put* the chair in the position of the children and you sit there, and I'm not an expert in this stuff, let me just say that right now that I'm not an expert, but there's a system, there's a whole cosmological sort of system thing and it's an ancient Chinese cosmological system sort of thing and I read the book, okay…and they tell you on page twenty-

seven, that a lot of what's goin' on here is intuitive…
like you've got all these positions and rules about what
goes where, and there's this thing called the *ch'i*, and
it's a big deal thing and you want to place stuff so that
the *ch'i* can move around the way it wants to move
around, but ya' don't want it to move too fast either,
and one thing influences another, and everything
influences everything else, and, the bottom line here,
and they're being very candid about this, is that
you've got to rely on your own intuition. And lucky for
me I'm an intuitive kind of guy kind of person, okay…
and you sort of have to play around with the whole
cosmological concept and find out what works for
you, and not every day is going to be the same…things
change…and that's what it's all about, things change,
and maybe one day the chair's going to work for you
better down over here and the next day it's going to
work better for you up over there in the position of
wealth, for example.

*(He indicates upstage left, thinks for a moment, then moves
the chair to a position upstage left in the position of wealth,
then crosses away from it, turns back and studies it, then
turns to the audience.)*

I'd like to start with an understanding that this doesn't
have anything to do with the sex thing or the gender
thing…I mean I'm a guy kind of person and all that,
but I'm not involved in any sort of relationship, sexual
or otherwise with anyone male, female, or otherwise,
and the main thing here is that I don't have any sex
drive, and I'll just tell ya' that right now, okay…none.
Absolutely none. And that didn't used to be the case
when I was writing poetry…because when I was
writing poetry I was controlled by relentless sexual
urges, sexual images goin' through my head all the
time, body-part kind of images, and since I've quit
writing poetry, that's all gone. And it's a lot better

now, really a whole lot better, and I figure that if you don't have any sex drive and aren't having any sexual relationships, then it means that the whole gender thing is irrelevant, and by saying that I'm not saying that I'm one of those cross-dressing kind of people, okay. I'm not saying that at all, and I just want to say right now that if the cross-dressing kind of lifestyle is something you're into then it's one-hundred-percent okay with me, because I think that everybody should be able to wear whatever they want to wear and be whatever kind of sex person they want to be, and whatever kind of racial-ethnic thing they want to be, Democrat, Republican, and if you want to make charitable contributions, okay…and if you don't want to…I mean, a whole lot of people are comin' on to ya' these days asking for charitable contributions, have you noticed this…and I'm one those kind of guys whose always willing to reach down into his pocket and pull out some change and give whatever I can to help another human being kind of person of whatever racial-ethnic-gender-socio-economic thing they're into…and I always give to organizations like Meals-on-Wheels…I *like* Meals-on-Wheels…I think the whole Meals-on-Wheels concept is an A-number-one kind of multicultural humanitarian transgender concept… and I like knowin' that I'm helping some old lady, or whatever, and you just never know…*you just never know* whether one of these days you just might *need* Meals-on-Wheels, and I'd like to know that they're still going to be around when the time comes.

(Pause as he moves around the space for a moment, looking things over)

I've been thinking about creating an indoor garden…a lot of different plants, a grow light coming down from the ceiling, roses, lavender, foxglove, a whole English cottage garden sort of thing…and I've been thinking about putting it over here in the position of knowledge

(Indicating)

…and then over here

(Indicating)

I'll have the books and the magazines, and up over here in the position of fame

(Indicating)

I'm going to keep the portfolio of high-quality blue-chip Fortune 500 stock certificates and high-yield bonds, and this is where I used to keep my poetry until I burned all of it last night, and over here in the position of marriage I'm going keep the cheese and crackers and tea bags and cocoa…the essential things…the alcohol…

(Beat, as he stops, looks around)

It's a funny thing being normal. All my life from babyhood on I was aware that I wasn't normal, and this can have a very disenfranchising effect on a person…you know you don't belong and you want to belong, at least you *think* you want to belong, because the adventure-and-romance video-and-film propaganda conglomerate is always tellin' ya' that you want to belong…and then there you are: *not* normal, *not* liked, *not* belonging, looking in through the window at the pretty party that's going on inside with all the pretty, nice, normal people to-ing-and-fro-ing and talking about their little normal things, and you're not one of them because you're not normal…and nobody wants to talk to you or look at you and you start to feel that you're invisible, which can give you a pretty bad attitude, okay…and your health suffers, and your nerves suffer, and your productivity suffers, and you think that if you could just write some really great poetry you wouldn't exactly be *normal*, but you'd be *special* and everyone would want to suck you off. And I went to college, okay, and I read Byron, and I read Keats and Shelley and Wordsworth and Coleridge and Whitman and Emily Dickinson and Anne Sexton and Allen Ginsberg and I even read some of those people who make absolutely no sense at all, okay… and they all thought that everyone was going to want to suck them off…and well, Ginsberg, okay, Whitman, okay, maybe everybody *did* suck them off…but I don't think any of the rest of them got sucked off…Byron maybe, Anne Sexton maybe…but I know for a fact that Coleridge spent his whole life jacking off and I used to do that, and I want to say that right now, I admit it, I used to engage in that kind of hand job kind of behavior when I was writing poetry and, now, since last night, I don't.

(Long beat)

It's better. Really, the whole thing's a whole lot better now, and for the whole day since waking up I've had a good appetite, I've had a good attitude, and I've been quietly reviewing the political scene, the Dow Jones and the NASDAQ scene, and the whole diversified-investment kind of thing, and even though at this present moment I don't have any capital that's in a liquid sort of investment-ready condition, I've been making a lot of plans about when I *do* have some capital that's in a liquid sort of investment-ready condition…

(Suddenly stomping on an ant)

Fucking ants! Fucking goddamned ants. You know, I had the place sprayed…last week…the whole perimeter was sprayed with a really dangerous toxic pesticide that was absolutely guaranteed to kill fleas and ants and roaches and a whole lot of other things including small children, and I had to leave the premises, I'm serious about this…I had to vacate the premises for twelve hours and then ventilate the premises for an additional twelve hours, and it's not like I leave food lying, around because I take most of my meals out, okay, down at the Taco Bell…chicken burrito supreme, that sort of thing…and a certain number of my calories are from alcohol, I don't try to hide that fact…

(He picks up the phone.)

Hello…Gabriella…how you doin'? This is Sparky, listen, I wanted to invite you to a party, ya' know what I mean? …Really…my place…really, I'm serious…I'm going to be having a few friends over, and I thought if you wanted to come over and join in on all the fun we're going to be having…

(He hangs up the phone.)

And my whole social life has been on the upswing, because now that I'm normal I'm doing the things that nice normal people do when they're normal, like I'm going to have a party tomorrow night, a very nice party, and I'm inviting a number of old friends and some new friends, a nice mixture of nice, normal people, some of whom know each other, some of whom don't know each other, and it's going to be one of those stand-up affairs, with some nice wine and cheese-and-crackers and a casual but special kind of ambiance, a kind of a see-and-be-seen sort of thing…

(He picks up the phone.)

Randy, guy, how 'ya doin'…it's me, Sparky…*Sparky Litman*, remember me, from the bowling league, you remember the bowling league? …Randy, listen, I'm going to be having a party over here at my place, one of those nice stand-up things with the wine and the cheese and the salted nuts, sort of a see-and-be-seen kind of meet-the-people kind of thing, completely nonthreatening…

(He listens for a moment.)

I don't know what kind of wine just yet, you know, some sort of selection of different kinds of interesting wines from around the world…

(He listens for a moment.)

Sure, you can taste them first if that's what you want, okay…it's going to be one of those nice wine-tasting, cheese-and-cracker-tasting sort of things, and you can bring your own, whatever, okay, no big deal…. Different people, Randy, just different people, okay, some of whom know each other, some of whom don't know each other, a nice selection of nice, normal people with the usual everyday selection of fears and neuroses….

(He hangs up the phone.)

And it makes me feel really good to be able to bring people together in a way that I didn't use to be able to do when I was a poet, because when you're a poet you have to spend all your time, every minute, sunup to sundown, being a poet, and it takes a whole lot of concentration to do that, because you've got to keep your mind wrapped around whatever painful, heart-rending kernel of truth you're trying to write a poem about, and you don't have any time to engage in a normal social life, and that's fine if you don't like people…but I like people, okay, all sorts of people, a lot of different, multicultural, transgender people…

(He picks up the phone.)

Jesse, this is Sparky…Sparky…Sparky Litman… Listen, Jesse, I'm having a party tomorrow night, because I'm not writing poetry anymore, and I'm inviting some people I know and some people I don't know to come on over and help me celebrate, and you're somebody I *don't* know, but you've come highly recommended, and I was wondering if you'd like to come on over, because it's going to be a very nice party, very nice, with a nice selection of wines from around the world…

(Beat)

Susan…Susan Milner…Susan Milner told me about you…she's a small woman, brown hair, says to say, "hi", she might be coming too…you don't think you know her…really…she said you were old friends… well, this could be a nice opportunity to meet her if you'd like, she's very nice, very small….

(He puts down the phone.)

And you can't always predict what kind of reaction you're going to get, because some people are going to say "yes" and some people are going to say "no," and I try not to take it too personally, because I've always tended to be overly sensitive about everything, like rejection, for example, which is something I know a lot about, because it's been a major theme in my life, and I have to be careful…and so I'm only inviting people I know or people who have been recommended by people I *do* know, no open-door policy, because I did my time, okay…during the Vietnam business…and I served in a special capacity in the intelligence arena, in an underground bunker beneath the airport of a major metropolitan American city, the name of which *to this day* I'm not at liberty to divulge…and during my years as a super-secret intelligence operative I was exposed to extremely sensitive top-secret kind of information, and you've got to be careful about who you associate with and who you invite into your home, because there are people *to this day* who are going around out there trying to get their hands on this extremely sensitive top-secret kind of information, and these are not nice people…these are nefarious, evil, dangerous, not particularly good-looking people, and they could be walkin' down the street *at any time* pretending to be lookin' for a party to go to, trying to pass themselves off as regular party-goin' kind of people, and a guy in a position such as myself has to be on his guard… which is one of the reasons I've tried to create this sort of oasis here…a quiet space, a safe, protected space with a secure perimeter, but an interesting space, a stimulating space, a space where you can feel the pulse of life, the flow of the *ch'i*, and right here in the center is the *ba-gua*.

(*He stands for a moment and studies the <D>ba-gua<MI>.*)

The *ba-gua* is the position of earth, the position of health, and it's the center and it's a special kind of sacred place, and every day I walk around the *ba-gua* twenty-seven times…clockwise twenty-seven times, because walking refreshes the *ch'i*, and helps to stimulate the flow of the *ch'i*, and I want my guests to experience the *ch'i* right when they come in the door, and they'll want to join in the flow of the *ch'i*, and I'm thinking about putting the food and drinks in the center, in the *ba-gua*, and the guests will move around the room in a clockwise direction and I'll be standing up here in the position of marriage

(*Indicates*)

…a symbol of union between me and my guests…and at some point after most of the guests have arrived I'll start moving around too, mixing and mingling, chitting and chatting, and, of course, there are going to be people who will want to make a late entrance.

(*He picks up the phone.*)

I was wondering if I could speak with Miss Turner… Miss Tina Turner…I want to invite her to a party I'm having, and you can tell her that my name is Sparky

Litman…S-P-A-R-K-Y L-I-T-M-A-N, and I'm one of her greatest fans, and I think that she's getting more beautiful and fabulous and sexy and wonderful every year, and I'm in love with her at a really deep level, that's sort of a cosmic kind of level, like a whole spiritual kind of love thing that's hard to define, because it's so deep and cosmic and spiritual that it's a religious kind of love, like some people have for the Virgin Mary.

(He puts down the phone.)

I think it would be nice to have music…and if you're going to have music you should have the best music, no imitations, and Tina's music comes straight from her gut and from her heart….

(He picks up the chair and moves it upstage center.)

Maybe Miss Turner would like to sit here in the position of fame….

(He sets the chair down, steps back and studies it.)

Maybe she would like to sit here when she's not singing and drink a little wine and eat some cheese-and-crackers and little wieners in sweet-and-sour sauce and talk to some of the nice, normal people who are going to be here and who will want to meet her and experience her life force…and some of them might want to tell her that they're wildly aroused by her and dream about her almost every night and are totally excited by the way she sings and moves around in that totally sexy, dirty-evil kind of way…and I've been under a lot of pressure lately, okay…a lotta stuff goin' on pertaining to my life-time goals and my precarious financial situation, and then last week I was walking along, and this was when I was still writing poetry and I was concentrating on my pain, trying to find the right words, the right images to describe the deep, deep hopelessness of my pain, and all of a sudden this woman walks over and starts givin' me the third degree about my dog taking a shit on her lawn...and I start tellin' her that I don't have a dog, and she starts yellin' at me, callin' me a spic, and it's, like, okay, I'm sayin' and I'm backin' away from her, and she's yellin' something about all you fuckin' spics comin' on up here lettin' your dogs shit on the nice, normal lawns, and the next thing I knew this neighbor guy comes out and *he* starts yellin' at me too, just because this woman's yellin' at me, and pretty soon they're chasing me down the street, yellin' at me about the dog I don't have, and this is in the same neighborhood that I've lived in my whole life...and okay...so maybe they've seen me goin' back and forth to the Taco Bell, ya' know what I mean...because I *do* go back and forth to the Taco Bell on a daily basis, two or three *times* on a daily basis, and the irony here is that just the other day this letter came in the mail from some genealogist kind of guy person who was trying to trace all the descendants of what turns out to be my grandfather's family tree...and the bottom line here, and I just want to be totally frank about this, is that my grandfather, my mother's father, the guy who was always referred to as "the Spaniard," ya' know what I mean...was really a Mexican Jew...and let me just say right now that I'm not circumcised, okay...we didn't know we were Jews, no one told us we were Jews, and nobody ever told us we were Mexican either, and the only thing grandpa ever knew was that he was born in L A...and so now I'm wanderin' around with this information that I don't exactly know what to do with, because, frankly, I'll tell ya', as far as I can figure I'm still the same mongrel-mix, chicken-burrito-eating American I always was...

(*He picks up the phone.*)

Hello, Gretchen…how ya' doin', Gretch, it's me, Sparky, long time no see, no talk…Sparky…*Sparky*…S-P-A-R-K-Y, listen, Gretch, you still single? …Look, Gretchen, I'm going to be having a little party over here at my place tomorrow night, and Miss Tina Turner's gonna be here, and I thought you bein' a real Tina Turner fan you'd want to be part of the crowd… Tina…Tina Turner…Tina Turner, Private Dancer, great legs, Ike and Tina, T-I-N-A T-U-R-N-E-R…and she's going to be here and she's gonna sing some of her favorite songs and talk to people, and it's going to be one of those stand-up kind of things…stand-up…nice wine, different kinds of imported and domestic cheeses and those nice little wieners in sweet-and-sour sauce, everybody walkin' around with the flow of the *ch'i*, trying not to spill anything…

(He puts down the phone.)

So I'm trying to be a little more open to people, a little more accommodating, and I'm going to try to be a little more understanding about them, because it's tough, ya' know what I mean…the whole life thing is a real tough thing to put a person through, and I didn't use to have a whole lot of sympathy for people when I was a poet, because you're not *supposed* to have a whole lot of sympathy for people when you're a poet, you're supposed to assault them, okay…you're supposed to brutalize them and shock them and make them think about something or have a revelation about something or at the very least *feel* something, preferably something really painful…and last night I was walking around, and it was late, real late, somewhere in the middle of the middle of a long, long, tortured, dark-night-of-the-soul kind of night, and I hadn't written shit, okay…not shit, not one crummy little stanza or verse or stinky little couplet or anything, and for a while I had the chair up here—

(He indicates.)

—sort of halfway between the position of marriage and the position of children, and you'd think that'd be a great place to sit, right? Creative, right? Fecundity, union, offspring…and I kept moving the chair around and I couldn't get comfortable, and I'm just new at this Chinese placement thing, okay…it's a whole new thing for me, and it's not like you're expected to get it all right off, because it's an art form itself, it's a spiritual sort of thing, and ya' gotta keep trying, ya' gotta keep playin' around with it, and so I kept moving the chair tryin' out different positions, and I couldn't find a single word that was worth writing down, not one, and I tried all of 'em and I moved 'em around and tried 'em in different combinations, old, tired, stinking, worn-out, overused words that I'm sick of and everybody else is sick of, and it started me thinking about when I used to spy on the Hungarian Air Force…and I mean this is the sort of thing I'm not supposed to talk about, because it's a secret kind of thing, and I guess they don't want anybody to know that they wasted a whole lot of money spying on the Hungarian Air Force…and I used to listen to these radio conversations that these pilot guys were having when they were up there flying around, and what these guys were doin' was talkin' in numbers, ya' know what I mean…like seventeen…thirty-three…eighteen…code word…code word…eighteen…thirty-two…forty-seven…code word… And I was supposed to listen to this stuff, and it wasn't like it was all nice and crystal clear…this was static, seriously un-Dolbyized static, and these Hungarian pilot guys were talkin' these numbers to each other in Hungarian, okay…Hungarian numbers, Hungarian code words, and I don't know any Hungarian, and they *knew* that we were listening to them, okay… they *knew* that, and so just to fuck with us they got

in their airplanes, and they had about three of 'em,
the whole lousy, stinking Hungarian air force had
about three old World War II kinda planes, and they
got up there on Monday, Wednesday, and Friday
mornings, and sometimes on Saturday afternoons,
but never on Tuesdays, Thursdays, or Sundays, and
never when it rained, because they couldn't fly in
the rain, and never at the end of the month, because
they ran out of their gas allotment by the end of the
month, and they were up there goin' code word, code
word, number, number, and there were these people,
okay…men and women kind of people, American
kind of cross-cultural transgender kind of very *quiet*
people who sat in the huge locked-up, super-secret,
acoustical-tiled, no-window, concrete-walled room
in the bunker underneath the major airport of the
major American city…and these people spent the
day poring over these printouts of number, number,
codeword, codeword, looking for correspondences
and configurations and repeated patterns, something
that would make it appear that somehow somewhere
something was making some sort of sense. And
no one knew Hungarian, okay…*I* didn't know any
Hungarian, the guy who intercepted the stuff didn't
know any Hungarian, none of the people who sat in
the huge, locked-up, super-secret, acoustical-tiled room
knew any Hungarian, because all of this was such a
big, special secret that the Central Intelligence people
wouldn't let anybody who *knew* Hungarian listen to
what the Hungarians were saying, because if they *knew*
Hungarian, they probably *were* Hungarian, and if they
were Hungarian then they were the enemy.

(Pause, as he picks up the chair and moves it down stage right and places it just so. He stands back and studies it.)

(Very calmly)

Here is knowledge.

(Beat)

Here is the place where the wisdom of the ancient peoples comes together, a place where you can experience the deeper understandings that have been passed down from generation to generation, and you can sit here… quietly…consciously… intentionally… and you can feel the movement of the *ch'i*, the wind and the water, the life force…and you can breathe the air…

(He does so.)

…slowly…quietly…consciously…intentionally… and contemplate the possibilities of where to place the chair, where to place the bed, where to place the bouquet of flowers and the light and the mirror to allow for the beneficial flow of the life-giving, beautiful *ch'i*….

(Suddenly stepping viciously on an ant)

Fucking ants! Fucking goddamn ants! And ya' know it pisses me off, because I spent one hundred thirty-seven dollars and eighty-three cents to have this outfit come out and spray the entire perimeter inside and out, the entire perimeter with this pesticide that has been banned, but this outfit is still using it…it's an underground kind of thing goin' on here, and you talk to somebody who talks to somebody else and then they drop ya' a note and make arrangements to come over for the "feasibility inspection" and ya' pay for this, ya' know, it's not cheap, one hundred thirty-seven dollars and eighty-three cents, and it's got a five-year guarantee, okay, that's what this guy said, five years, and he had these assistants, these guys all done up in these chemical warfare sort of suits, and they sprayed this totally toxic, cancer-producing pesticide all along the perimeter inside and out, and I've still got ants, whole platoons of 'em, battalions, and it's going on all over the neighborhood, that's the problem, the fucking neighborhood, and the filth that lives here, but it's all I've ever been able to afford as a poet, because you don't get to live in the real, hoity-toity, ant-free neighborhoods when you're a poet, you gotta live in the kind of neighborhoods where ya' got a lot of these people sittin' around in their homes at night, behind their barricaded doors, eatin' their Frito-Lays, watching the ants march across the room, and it's these same people who are watching all of those movies, you know what I mean, every night they're watching these romance-and-adventure propaganda movies, and now they don't just go *out* to watch 'em, they watch 'em *in* their homes, *in their homes*, night after night, munchin' away on their Frito-Lays, ants crawling around all over the place, and here I'm tryin' to have this party tomorrow night, tryin' to have a nice, tasteful, modest-but-not-too-modest kind of evening where people can meet and mingle and relate to one another on a one-to-one interactive kind of basis, and that can be kind of scary, okay…kind of scary for a lot of people, including myself, to try to relate to another person on a one-to-one interactive kind of basis, and that's what I'd like to be able to do without having to deal with a whole bunch of fuckin' stupid, goddamned fuckin' stupid ants!!

(He steps on another ant and then violently stomps all over a bunch of them. There's a pause, as he crosses, picks up the chair and moves downstage and sits on it, then pulls it closer to the audience to talk confidentially.)

Things were goin' pretty well for me until the whole puberty-adolescent episode, the seventh-grade hormone episode… And I was a pretty quiet kinda kid, because for the most part people made fun of me for one reason or another, and ya' just learn to keep quiet when people make fun of you, and this was during the period when everyone was getting their mannerisms down right, ya' know what I mean…like how you stood and how you walked and how you moved your arms and hands around and got the whole thing synchronized with what you're doing and saying…and I was having a pretty bad time gettin' the whole thing down right, okay…I was havin' a pretty bad time with the whole hand, eye, arm, leg, foot, mouth coordination thing, and, I'll tell ya' right now, I was spending most of my time lookin' at Mary Beth Latimore…three rows over, pink angora sweater, little blonde ponytail, Mary Beth Latimore, who spent most of her time looking at everyone else except me. And I'd smile at her, like I'd give her a real nice I-really-like-you kind of sincere-genuine kind of smile, and she'd look away real fast and pretend that she didn't see me, do you get this picture? And I was getting kind of desperate, okay… because the whole puberty-adolescent thing was goin' on and everybody was getting involved in boy-girl kind of relationships, going to parties, makin' out in the corner, stuff like that, and I was never invited to any of the parties and I never got to make out in the corner and develop a boy-girl kind of relationship, so I decided that the only thing to do in my situation was to ask Mary Beth Latimore out on a date…like a first-date sort of arrangement…and I thought that the Ringling Brothers Barnum and Bailey Circus would be a fun, wholesome, sophisticated sort of thing to do for a first-date kind of experience, and we could get there on the bus, and you had to think about that sort of thing in the seventh grade, the whole transportation issue, and we'd eat cotton candy and watch the aerialist people and the lion tamer people and maybe hold hands and she'd get to have the opportunity to realize what a really pretty decent kind of modest kind of guy I was. And I was saving my money, okay…the little bit I could scrape together from my crappy little nickel-and-dime allowance, and I was tryin' to get up my nerve to ask her, and it was scary, because I'd never really talked to her, and I knew I was never going to be able to talk to her, and so I decided to write her a note. And that was scary too because you gotta get the words just right, sort of easy-goin' but not too easy-goin', and after I'd written about thirty-seven drafts I finally had something I thought was really pretty nice, friendly yet respectful, not too formal, not too casual, and I put it in an envelope and carefully wrote her name and carried it around for a few days and took it out and looked at it a lot, because I didn't have the nerve to walk over and give it to her…and it got to be about two days before the circus, okay…and it was gettin' to the point where if I didn't give it to her it was going to be too late, and it was just before lunch, and the bell rang, and everyone was gettin' their stuff together and I held my breath and got up and tried to walk over to her real cool and casual and I was sweating, I admit that…I was sweating and my hands were kind of shaking, and I couldn't look at her, because I was too embarrassed, and so there I was all of a sudden standing right in front of Mary Beth Latimore staring down at the front of her pink angora sweater…and I handed her the note…and then I looked up and she was giving me one of these "why-are-you-bothering-me-you-repulsive-piece-of-shit" contemptuous kind of looks, d'you know this kind of look…and she took the note and opened it and read it and started laughing hysterically and ran over to Cynthia Petersberg and showed it to her, and they both started laughing hysterically, and then Cynthia Petersberg took it and showed it to every single other person in the entire class, and they all started laughing hysterically, and these are the same people who are running around today with big fat oversized 401K plans, okay…these are the same people who grew up all nice and normal with all the right mannerisms and the right voice and the whole social know-how thing at their disposal, and they all started putting handfuls of their discretionary income into big fat oversized 401K plans, and I never had any discretionary income, okay…I never had the opportunity to *be* in one of those employment situations where you could have discretionary income and put handfuls of cash into a big fat oversized 401K plan…

(He picks up the phone.)

Hello. This is Mr Sparky Litman. And I'm interested in getting one of those floral arrangement kind of things, maybe a couple of those floral arrangement kind of things…for a party, one of those nice stand-up affairs, hors d'oeuvres, wine, some nice flowers here and there, adding a little color and scent, creating an aura of exotic beauty and sensuous smells…

(He puts down the phone, then picks it up again.)

Hello. This is Mr Sparky Litman. And I'm interested in getting an assortment of canapés, some of those little cracker sort of things, little cheese spread, olives with the pimentos, that sort of thing…

(He puts down the phone.)

A little bit of preparation can prevent a lot of heartache. I want to say that again: A little bit of preparation can prevent a lot of heartache. And the thing is I didn't used to believe in preparation, okay…I believed in spontaneity…I thought that spontaneity was the morally and existentially superior way to go and that to plan for something merely reinforces the prevailing mythology that there is something to plan *for*…and, of course, I knew then and I know now that there isn't *really* anything to plan *for*…but what I didn't know then and what I do know now is that it's better to *prepare* for something even if you know it's never going to happen…because it gives you a feeling that something *is* going to happen, and if you just sit around all day being spontaneous nothing ever *does* happen, and then you're left sitting home alone with the ants, nursing a big dose of heartache.

(He picks up the phone.)

This is Mr Sparky Litman again…say, you don't have any of those puff pastry things that have those kind of nice, mystery fillings on the inside, those kind of things that you can't quite figure out what you're eating, but they're good anyway and they make nice little conversation-starters?

(He puts down the phone; there's a beat.)

I thought maybe I was going to die last week. I just had this queasy sort of gnawing-in-my gut kind of feeling that I was going to die, and I wasn't too sure whether it was going to be from natural causes or unnatural causes…but I felt like I was coming down with a really bad case of terminal mortality, and I'm ready, okay… Death is not a problem for me, I am not one of these people who has a problem with death and spends a whole lot of time all tied up in a knot about death, because *life* is the problem, okay…*death* is *not* the problem, *life* is the problem, and I've excavated an area down in the basement over here in the position of the children…

(He indicates.)

…and it's where I'm going to be buried when the time comes, and it's all part of a very nice, very tasteful burial chamber that I've created down there for my family…each person's ashes at rest in a vessel that is appropriate for the personality and the occasion…all carried out in a nice Egyptian motif…

(He indicates.)

…and my grandmother the Norwegian is here

(He indicates.)

…and my grandfather, the Mexican Jew from L A, is here

(He indicates.)

…and over here are our neighbors, Doris and Sam Smedly, who, and I'll be brutally honest here, I never really liked…there wasn't much really to like about old Doris and Sam, but they used to hang out a lot with Mom and Dad, drinkin' and cussin', and gettin' into political sort of arguments with each other, and there was some kind of a sex thing goin' on between Doris and Mom, and Doris was always pawin' around at her, holding her hand, kissin' her and stuff, and you certainly couldn't blame old Doris, because Sam was one of those kind of guys who had a permanent really bad body odor kind of problem goin' on…and they'd watch T V and drink and argue and sooner or later Doris would fall asleep on the living room sofa, and at one point she moved some of her stuff into the spare room and started sleeping there, and not too long after that Sam moved some of his stuff in there too, and they never really left.

(Beat)

I never intended to be a hero, okay…I never had any fantasies about bein' a hero or had any plans to go out and do something that would make me a hero, I was just tryin' to do my best to be a regular kind of guy, writin' my poetry, sellin' Electrolux vacuum cleaners door to door, and I just want to say that this is a quality product…but then time and circumstance, and this is the thing, time and circumstance, it wasn't a planned sort of thing, okay…your country calls on you, and you do what you have to do, and they called on me, and we were at war against the so-called enemy in Vietnam, and I was called and I responded, and it didn't surprise me that they put me into the intelligence arena, okay… because I've got a first rate-kind of intelligence kind of brain, and the Army personnel people sensed that right off, and they pulled me aside and asked me very discreetly if I wanted to be involved in the intelligence arena, and I told them that if that's what my country wanted me to do…

(Beat)

So they sent me to spy school, and this is something I'm not supposed to talk about, that was somewhere in the middle of New Mexico, except I don't know exactly where, because they flew us to Albuquerque in the middle of the night and put us on these buses that had the windows painted over so we couldn't see where we were going, and it was me and a bunch of other guys, who ended up locked up together in these old World War II Army barracks that were surrounded by fourteen-foot-high electrified barbed-wire fences…and all day long, starting at five A M in the morning, they taught us the stuff that we needed to know about being a spy…like the secret hand signals, what to wear, who you could talk to, who you couldn't talk to, number, number, code word, code word, that kind of thing… and there was a lot of messin' around goin' on there, okay, a lot of queer stuff going on there, guys jackin' each other off and stuff, and at first, ya' know, I wasn't going to get involved in that sort of thing…but it was wartime…and there was a lot of stress and you never knew if you were going to get called to the front lines and have your head blown off, and you'd get back to the barracks after a long day of number, number, code word, code word, and there wasn't a whole hell of a lot ya' could do except smoke dope and drink a lot of tequila and get naked, and one thing led to another, and I'm only human, okay…and a lot of these guys were like that, kinda lonely, dealin' with the whole war thing, the whole life and death thing, just jackin' each other off, servin' their country...

(Beat)

And I've kept all of my medals, the special service, the duty above-and-beyond, and when you serve behind enemy lines they give you this very special medal that's got this fancy oak leaf cluster thing and a big, red ribbon, and they didn't tell me at first that they were going to send me behind enemy lines, they didn't mention that...and of course, they can't tell you a whole lot, because then it wouldn't be secret, and the idea behind the whole thing is secrecy, okay...and so one day they pulled me aside and started talkin' about how they needed a real special kind of guy, a dedicated, discreet, can-do kind of guy...somebody who could penetrate into the heart of the whole huge Red Commie Empire and figure out what, if anything, was goin' on.

(Beat)

Well, I wasn't so sure, I mean, you know...I wasn't exactly real crazy about the whole idea, and I told them quite frankly about Mom and Dad, and how I didn't think it would work out real well for me to be too far away from 'em, because they were gettin' along in years and needed someone to be there, and my parents, you know, god love 'em, didn't understand a goddamn thing, not a single goddamn thing...and you couldn't *tell* poor old Mom and Dad what was goin' on, god love 'em, and they were pretty dumb, I'll just have to say that, Mom and Dad were pretty dumb, and I don't mean that in a negative kind of way, just in a loving *objective* kind of way...and they tried, you know, and Mom was, well, you know, she had a mental condition and spent a lot of time hiding out under her bed…and it's not like I ever did real well in school, either, because I wasn't normal, and I knew I wasn't normal, and Mom and Dad knew I wasn't normal and they thought it was *their* fault, and frankly it *was* their fault, I'll just have to say that…because *they* weren't normal either, and neither were Doris and Sam Smedly or anybody else in the whole neighborhood for that matter, and the fact is that I didn't have one single, normal role model, not *one single, normal* role model, and so there I was with the Central Intelligence people tellin' me that I was exactly the right kind of special sort of anonymous, confused-looking kind of guy they'd been lookin' for.

(Beat)

You can appeal to my ego. I'll admit that. You say the right kinda stuff and I'll do just about anything, because I'm insecure, okay…and I've always been insecure, and I've always wanted to be liked by people and be special and you can really mess around with people like me…you can really screw people like me over, and the next thing I knew they were fixin' me up with this whole wardrobe of wash-and-wear polyester shirts and underpants and a pair of shoes that looked like a pair of shoes, except the right shoe was really a secret radio transmitter-receiver kind of thing… and then they gave me a one-way ticket on the Trans-Siberian Railroad, that I was supposed to take from this place called Nahodka to Moscow, eight days through the heart of the Red Commie Soviet Empire, and the whole thing was about trucks…because they thought that the trucks were being made someplace outside of Budapest, and they thought that they were being shipped by train through Poland and then traveled in caravans toward Minsk, but once the trucks left Minsk, no one could figure out what exactly was happening to them, except they thought maybe the Soviet Commies were shipping them to the Chinese Commies and the Chinese Commies were shipping 'em to the Commies in North Vietnam, big deal, okay, big international wartime political deal goin' on, and they wanted me to see what I could find out.

(Beat)

So the plan was that I was supposed to go ridin' along on the train, real cool, real noncommittal, pretending that I'm just one of those goin'-for-a-ride-on-the-Trans-Siberian-Railroad tourist kind of guys…lookin' out the window, chattin' it up with the other tourist kind of people, keepin' my eyes open to see if there were any trucks headin' to China or overhear any conversations about trucks heading to China, and in general keep an eye out for anything else that was suspicious, like any sort of unexplained counterintelligence espionage kind of activities, and I'm thinkin' ya' know that I don't speak any Russian, okay…and I'm not so sure if I'd recognize any sort of unexplained counterintelligence espionage kind of activity if I saw it, ya' know what I mean…I mean, does it look any different than what's going on all the rest of the time? So then they give me a ruble, ya' know, a Russian ruble, picture of Lenin, about the size of a quarter, and I'm thinkin' like maybe it's for makin' a phone call home…but then they tell me that they want me to give it to this guy named Boris, who's going to meet me in Moscow, and they show me that there's a secret little compartment sewn into my polyester underpants where I can keep the ruble and guard the ruble, and I wasn't supposed to show it to anybody or tell anybody about it until I got to Moscow where this guy named Boris was going to meet me at the train station and whisper number, number, code word, code word, and then I was supposed to whisper code word, code word, number, number, and then he was supposed to say, "Welcome, comrade brother," and then I was supposed to give him the ruble. So I started to ask a few questions…and they told me I wasn't allowed to ask any questions, and I'm thinking like what if this ruble thing is some sort of explosive device, ya' know, like maybe they're really sending me off on some sort of suicide bombing mission or something, and I tried to explain that I had a certain right to know, and they said that I didn't have any right to know anything about anything and that the whole thing was super top-secret and I was just supposed to shut up and do what I was told.

(Beat)

I mean, it's okay, ya' know…you can only assume that somebody somewhere knows what in the hell they're doin', and I was fully aware that I was just a pawn in the military-industrial-espionage complex, and it's then that I started having the serious acid-reflux indigestion that I'd never had before that point in time, and it's not like I had a choice about any of this, okay…I mean, these were orders, this was the army, this was wartime, this was the enemy, this was the objective, and I was Communications Specialist First Class Sparky Litman, and I was the man who they called on to get the job done.

(Long beat, as he moves the chair closer to the audience and leans in to talk very confidentially.)

It was winter, okay…and they bundled me up in this Eskimo kind of jacket and gave me some luggage and a camera and a passport that had my picture in it but with a different name that was hard to pronounce… and then they put me on a plane for Tokyo where I stayed for two days and then got on a Japanese ship that took me to this place called Nahodka that's north of Vladivostok where you catch the train…and it was cold, okay…real cold, like forty-seven degrees below

zero cold, and it was snowin', and I was scared, and
I'll just say that right now, because I was pretty sure
that at any moment some sort of ugly-lookin' K G
B kind of operative person was goin' to come along
and hold a gun to my head and take me off to some
sort of Siberian torture chamber...and so I'm goin'
along tryin' to act like a simple-minded tourist kind
of guy takin' a nice trip in minus forty-seven-degree
weather...and they show me to this train compartment,
and it's like one of those European trains with four
people in a compartment and there were these two big
Russian soldier guys and an old, old, old Russian crone
kind of lady, and I sat down, and everybody started
noddin' and smilin' and I started noddin' and smilin',
and they all started talking in Russian, and this one
soldier guy offers me a drink from his bottle of vodka
and I'm thinkin' that ya' know it's a friendly kind of
gesture and so I take a little drink and thank him and
he urges me to take some more and I do and then the
soldier guy passes the bottle to the old lady and she
drinks a little and they keep passin' this bottle around,
and then another bottle, and this is pretty much what
went on for the next eight days, okay...and this was a
Red Commie Soviet Empire train...I mean, it wasn't
exactly one of these scenic-cruiser-dome-car-nice-linen-
napkins-with-a-bar-car-in-the-rear sort of trains...
it was one of those kind of trains that barely had any
heat, for example, and there was about eighty feet of
snow outside and ice on the windows, and you'd sit
there rockin' back and forth drinkin' vodka, noddin'
and smilin', tryin' to keep warm, and three times a
day you'd have the pleasure of going down to the
so-called dining car where the only thing they served
was tongue. Beets and tongue. Potatoes and tongue.
Pimentos and tongue. Green-yellow weedy mystery
vegetables and tongue...and after a while you'd sort
of start to wonder: What in the hell are they doin' with

the *rest* of the animal, huh? Who's gettin' to eat that, huh? And it's not that you could even *tell* what *kind* of animal it was…it was just tongue, okay, fat, ugly, pink, pulled-out-by-the-roots tongue, and at one point it sort of occurred to me that maybe it wasn't even *animal* tongue…maybe it was dead human capitalist pig *spy* tongue, ya' know what I mean? And I wasn't sleepin' very well to begin with, because every night at exactly 0130 A M in the morning I had to get up and go down to what they called the toilet, which was one of those holes-in-the-floor sort of deals that ya' gotta squat over when the time comes…and I stood there and took off my shoe that was really a transmitter-receiver and radioed back to the underground bunker that I hadn't seen any trucks, because most of the time you couldn't see out the windows because of the ice and snow, and I hadn't heard anyone talking about any trucks either, because, let's face it, I don't speak any Russian, okay…I don't speak any Russian or Hungarian or Polish or Czechoslovakian or Serbo-Croatian, and there was this woman in dark glasses who started followin' me around, and she was a knockout drop-dead fasten-your-seat-belts kind of woman, nice legs, nice thighs, nice calves, nice ankles, real red lipstick, real thick and wet. And she started to make it a point to sit across from me in the dining car, and I'm just a modest kind of guy, okay, and I'm not used to women payin' a whole lot of attention to me, because they never *have* paid a whole lot of attention to me, and this woman was makin' me real nervous because I'm a spy, okay, and I'm on a top-secret intelligence mission, and this woman was pretending to read this book, and it was one of those big thick Russian novel sort of books with Cyrillic kind of letters all over the front cover, but the point is that she wasn't actually *reading* the book… she was just *pretending* to read the book while the whole time she was peekin' around at me, checkin' me out, watchin' me real closely as I was starin' out the window lookin' for trucks…and they warned me about this kind of person, okay…they showed me actual pictures of this kind of person, and told me about how this kind of person operated, and how this kind of person would lead you on with alcohol and drugs and red lipstick…and so I'd try to make sure that I sat in a different place at every meal…kind of moved around a bit, tryin' to keep her guessin', but she was smooth, okay…smooth, slick, professional, cold-blooded, and dangerous, and every time she'd find a place somewhere within eyeshot of where I was sittin', *every time*…and if she was sittin' at a table at one end of the car and I came in and sat down at a table at the other end of the car, she'd get up and move over by me, and then one night I look up and find her sittin' right next to me, and she looks at me and licks her lips and gives me one of those I-know-what-you-want kind of smiles, and I'm scared, okay…I just want to say that right now that I was scared and even under normal conditions I'd have been scared, and I'm thinkin' ya' know that this woman is working for the other side…I mean, let's face it right now, this woman is some sort of Russian secret service counterintelligence espionage kind of agent sort of woman and she knows who I am, she knows that I'm Communications Specialist Sparky Litman First Class, and she knows that I'm here on some sort of super-secret special sort of assignment, and she knows that she's got ways of making me talk.

(Beat)

So, she pulls out a pack of those ugly little black Sobrane cigarettes and asks me if I'd like a smoke… in English, she says this in English, kind of heavily accented English, but not exactly Russian-accented English, but more sort of Eastern European sort of accented English, and she's lickin' her lips and smilin' and then she sort of crosses her legs, you know how women do that, cross their legs real sort of slow and dirty…and then she moves closer to me and tells me that her name is Eva and that I shouldn't be afraid.

(Suddenly stamps viciously on a bunch of ants)

Fucking ants! Fucking goddamn ants! You can't win. There's no fuckin' hope. Fuckin' everywhere, and it doesn't make any difference what ya' try to do…

(He stomps around some more, then stops and picks up the phone, very irritated.)

Hello, this is Mr Sparky Litman, and I want to express my extreme dissatisfaction with your services. One hundred thirty-seven dollars and eighty-three cents! *One hundred thirty-seven dollars and eighty-three cents!* That's what I paid, *One hundred thirty-seven dollars and eighty-three cents!* And I *still* have ants, millions of ants, and I am having a party tomorrow night, and a number of very nice, very attractive, very clean people are going to be here, including Miss Tina Turner, who will be providing entertainment in her own unique, inimitable style, and I want you to come over here right now, this minute, this absolute minute, and bring your men and your equipment, and I want you to spray every square inch, and I want you to spray until *every single, solitary, wretched, filthy, disgusting, little ant is dead! Dead! Dead!*

(He slams down the phone, walks back to the chair, picks it up, moves it, stands there and takes a deep breath or two, slowly calms down, and then sits and then pulls the chair up closer to the audience.)

So, this Eva woman offers me a Sobrane, okay…and I say, sure, and I take it, and then she pulls out one of those fancy Dunhill lighters and lights mine and lights hers, and I take a drag and start coughin' real bad 'cause I don't smoke, but I wanted to play like I was real cool…and she starts laughin' and all of sudden I realize she's got her hand on my thigh…and I'm just a guy, okay…I'm just a human being kind of guy person, and I never had what you'd call a real sex life, a normal kind of boy-girl kind of sex life even though I had all of the usual sort of urges and some pretty unusual sort of urges, and she starts kind of feelin' me up, ya' know what I mean…and I'm gettin' aroused, okay… it's a natural kind of response, and she's gettin' her hand up there somehow or another, and she's kind of rubbin' it around, and I was tryin' to be cool, because there's this conductor kind of guy, who's a pretty scary-lookin' kind of guy, who comes along every hour or so checkin' the passports, and you could see him comin' on down the aisle, and this Eva woman's got her hand in my lap, and I've got a serious erection, okay…a *real, real* serious erection and she's rubbin' it and lickin' her lips and crossin' her legs and tellin' me how big it is, which it's not, and I'll just say that right now…I mean it's not exactly little or anything, it's a pretty regular-size kind of penis thing, and this scary-lookin' conductor guy's comin' down the aisle, and this Eva woman is rubbin' it harder and harder and faster and faster…and this is one of the reasons I started to write poetry…because of the frustration…because I've never been successful with women, and I'd never, up until that time in my life, had regular normal boy-girl kind of sexual relations with a woman…and so there was this woman comin' on to me in a serious sort of way, and we're sitting there on the Trans-Siberian Railroad and the conductor was comin' down the aisle, and this woman *knew* I was a spy, and *I* knew that *she* was a spy, and she knew what *I* was doin', and I knew what *she* was doin', and I knew that she wasn't really interested in me, okay, I knew that she wasn't really turned on to me, she just wanted my secrets, that was the only thing she was interested in, and I wanted her, and I'd just like to say that right now, because I was seriously excited by this woman, seriously aroused by this woman, because she was a beautiful-angelic-earth-goddess-Marlene-Dietrich kind of woman and I was falling in love…at that moment, it was love, true love, and my heart was pounding, and she was rubbing my thing, which was getting bigger and bigger and harder and harder than it had ever been in my entire life up to that time, and I'm not one of those kind of guys who just thinks about sex, okay…I think about love…I think about love and the whole beautiful heart-body-and-soul package, and I'm like reaching over there getting my hand up under her skirt, sort of a reciprocal kind of thing going on here, ya' know what I mean…and I'm startin' to get a real good feel up there, and I figure out pretty quickly that she's not wearin' any underpants, and she's like all wet and frothy and breathin' hard and smilin' and laughin' and things are gettin' real serious now, and I'm gettin' real worked up, and she's getting real worked up, and both of us have completely forgotten about the scary-lookin' conductor kind of guy who all of a sudden is standin' there, and he's watchin' us, and we just keep on goin' for it, and this Eva woman is starting to moan and sigh, and some of the other passengers have started to look and a few of 'em have stood up and come on over to stand around and catch the action, and she's unzipped my pants and pulled out my big, huge, enormous, throbbing penis thing, and she's pumpin' it and pumpin' it and she's going "yes, yes, yes, yes, yes…" and I'm feelin' like I can't hold it a second longer and just as I feel her insides start heavin' and quakin' like they're about to explode, I blow my wad all over the fucking train.

(Long pause as he moves the chair, pauses, sits on it, then pauses.)

I wasn't really planning on having a career in the military. I mean I knew I wouldn't be any good at that kind of thing, and *they* should have known that I wouldn't be any good at that kind of thing, and so there I was in the middle of Siberia with my dick hanging out and this scary-lookin' conductor guy is smilin' and laughing and breakin' out the vodka and this Eva woman has disappeared down the aisle, and I'm sort of tryin' to put myself back together when I realize that the ruble is gone, just gone. And I start searchin' around, thinkin' it might have fallen on the floor or somethin', and it only takes me a couple a seconds to realize that this Eva woman, the enemy counterintelligence agent, has taken it, and that's what this whole thing was all about, to distract me so she could get her hands on the ruble, and now it's in the hands of the enemy and I don't have anything to hand over to the guy in Moscow when he says number, number, code word, code word, and this is trouble, okay…this is big, huge, major, bad trouble, and I'm going to end up in front of a firing squad or something worse, and I panicked…and I just want to say that right now that I did not handle this in a cool, calm, professional, James Bond kind of manner, I started screaming,

(And he does.)

"Where's the fucking ruble! Where's the fucking ruble!" And I started trying to run down the aisle to find this Eva woman, and these other people are all blocking my path, okay, like they're not gonna let me through, and they're all drinkin' and laughin' and it's like they're in on the whole thing, like everybody on the train is in on this whole thing, everybody in the whole Soviet Commie empire is in on this thing, and this Eva woman has disappeared. Gone. Lost. Nowhere. Never to be seen again.

(Long beat)

You can begin to get the picture. I can tell, ya' know, that you're beginning' to really get the idea here of what it's been like for me, and I'm not complaining, I want to make that real clear right up front, that I'm not complaining, okay…ya' just start learnin' when you're real young that you're a dupe. I mean, that's what I was learnin', and that's what life was teachin' me, that I was one of those people who was born to be a dupe, somebody you could really take for a ride, because I never learned how to play the game, okay. I wasn't playin' the game, I didn't even know that there *was* a game…I was just innocent and stupid and terrified, the kind of guy who doesn't realize that everyone else is into something that requires some sort of *strategy*, ya' know what I mean? I didn't have a strategy. I didn't have a plan. I didn't know I needed one. And it turns out that there weren't any trucks, okay…it turns out that the Commies barely had any trucks, because they spent all their money on missiles and tanks, and the Central Intelligence people knew this, they knew this all along, but they wanted me to *think* that this whole thing was all about trucks, because it turns out they *wanted* the Commies to get the ruble, okay… they actually *admitted* this to me that they *wanted* the Commies to get the ruble, because there were secret *plans* of something big and important and classified top-secret top-secret microscopically engraved around the picture of Lenin…which was information that the Central Intelligence people just *happened* to *plant* in the *ear* of one of their operatives who they also knew was a *double agent* who would tell the Commies anything that he found out about, which included the fact that I was carrying this ruble with the secret plans in my underpants… But the plans were a fraud, okay…the plans were a red herring, okay…and they put me on the train knowing that the Commies knew who I was and what I was doing and that they'd drug me or something or kill me or something, and they'd get the ruble and think that they'd really gotten something big and important, and all along it was all part of big fat United States of America trap... And *they* were a dupe, and *I* was a dupe, and ultimately *everybody* in the whole entire world was a dupe.

(Beat)

So then they gave me a medal...for "valor and courage behind enemy lines" ...and Mom and Dad were real proud, because it was the first time in my whole life that I'd ever done something that they could be proud of, and it's not like I could really *tell* anybody about what I actually *did* to get the medal for valor and courage behind enemy lines... And it was then that I started staying awake at night, because I was afraid to go to sleep, because whenever I closed my eyes angry little voices started talking to me in my head, little voices speaking in little rhymed couplets all night long, and my appetite started going, and I'll tell you right now that there are a whole lot people who I really admire who killed themselves in one way or another... like Jackson Pollock...Jackson Pollock drank himself into a stupor and drove into a tree, and Mark Rothko drank himself into a stupor and slashed his wrists and bled to death, and the thing is I drink, okay...but I don't drink myself into a stupor...I just drink until the voices inside my head either take over completely or disappear completely...

(Suddenly, furiously starts stepping on ants, shouting)

Fucking ants! Fucking goddamned fucking fucking goddamned ants!

(In a frenzy, he picks up the chair and starts smashing the ants with it, pounding it against the floor over and over

until it breaks apart. Long beat as he regains his composure and moves downstage.)

I went down into the basement last night.

(Beat)

And I was lookin' things over and thinkin' about Mom and Dad and Grandma and Grandpa and the whole mortality situation, the whole life-and-death sort of thing…and I was thinking about the fact that everybody in the extended family unit is dead except me…I'm the last one…and I'm the only person who really knew them, because they didn't exactly have a lot of friends, in fact they didn't have *any* friends, and I didn't exactly know them real well either, okay…I mean, at one point or another we all lived in the same house and ate at the same table, and there was the whole sort of genetic thing going on, the whole D N A sort of thing, but you kinda got the feeling that nobody really *wanted* to get to know anybody real well, because they spent a lot of time yellin' at each other, and Mom couldn't think very well, couldn't figure stuff out real well, but she always tried to see to it that I got a good little breakfast and had a little peanut butter sandwich and an orange in a little bag to take to school for lunch…

(He gets teary-eyed, almost starts crying, and then holds back.)

And Dad was always wantin' to play catch with me… but I didn't want to play catch with him, because I couldn't catch…and he'd say that I'd never be *able* to catch unless I *tried* to catch, and I didn't care whether I could catch or not, and he'd get pissed, and then he'd start yellin' at me, and then Mom would start yellin' at him, and then he'd start yellin' at her, and then I'd go hide in my room, and they'd go on yellin' at each other, and how are ya' supposed to get to know anybody in that sort of environment, you know what I mean? I mean, *I did not know these people*. They were my parents, fine…they were Doris and Sam the neighbors who I didn't like very much, fine…they were my grandfather the Mexican Jew from L A and my grandmother the Norwegian, and *I did not know these people! Who were these people?!* And everybody's goin' on these days about *their* heritage, and *their* culture, and *their* traditions and history and people, and how special their people are, and my people weren't special, they weren't special at all, they were just unhappy, scared, terrified, lost, little people…and every night after Mom and Dad and Doris and Sam and Grandpa the Mexican Jew had pretty much passed out, Granny the Norwegian and I would sit up and watch wrestling matches on T V…which I pretty much hated, but Granny wanted to watch 'em, and I was the kind of kid who wanted to make his poor old confused granny happy, and so we'd watch wrestling, and she'd sit there rocking back and forth saying,

(Mimicking, distressed Norwegian)

"Vhy, vhy, vhy d'ese men kill each other…vhy, vhy, vhy?" And then she'd go on watching while these guys kept pounding away at each other, and she'd be shaking her head and beating her breast, saying, "Vhy, Vhy, Vhy d'ese men kill each other…vhy, vhy, vhy?" And I'd tell her, ya' know, like Granny, okay, like maybe we could change the channel, ya' know what I mean, like there's a whole lot of other, better stuff goin' on, and so I'd try to change the channel, but she wouldn't let me, and then she'd stare at the screen some more going, "Vhy, Vhy, Vhy d'ese men kill each other…vhy, vhy, vhy?"

(Beat)

So I was thinkin' that maybe tomorrow night, like when the people come to the party that maybe at some point they might like to come on downstairs and pay their respects to the dearly departed…and this could be sort of an optional kind of thing, okay…like maybe at some point after Miss Tina Turner has sung a few songs, and there's a little break for more conversation, another glass of wine, I could sort of casually mention to a few people that I'd like to introduce them to my extended family unit…and I'd invite them downstairs and show them around, and the whole place is lookin' real nice down there, okay…candles and incense, and everybody's urn is set out real nicely right here in the *ba-gua*

(Indicating center stage)

…the center, the earth, the position of health…

(Then indicating specifically and reverently)

…Mom and Dad…Grandma and Grandpa…Doris and Sam Smedly…

(Beat)

And I thought I could introduce my friends to them and tell people their names, sex, date of birth, date of death, country of origin, some brief biographical information…because the thing is, I never used to bring any of the kids from school home, okay…I never used to do that, because I didn't want them to meet my parents…and I didn't want them to meet my Grandpa and Grandma or Doris and Sam, because I was ashamed of them, and I just want to admit that…I was ashamed of my Mom and Dad and Grandpa and Grandma and poor old dumb Doris and Sam, and I never brought anybody home to meet them and I tried to pretend that I didn't even know them…in fact I *didn't* know them, I didn't know them at all, but you don't *realize* that while they're still alive, you don't *think* about that kind of stuff while they're still alive, and now that they're dead ya' realize that *you do not know these people*! And there they are down in your basement and you don't know who in the hell they are, and when they were alive you were ashamed of them, and it was a pretty crappy thing to do now, wasn't it? A pretty fucking crappy thing to do, and I was that kind of guy, okay...I was that kind of crappy, selfish, ashamed-of-my-people kind of guy, and it's sad, pretty fuckin' pathetically fuckin' sad...and I'm thinking now that it'd be pretty damned nice of me to introduce Mom and Dad and the whole extended family unit to these people who are comin' to this party sort of thing tomorrow night...sort of a pay-our-respects kind of thing, a moment of silence kind of thing, a little way for me to ask Mom and Dad to forgive me, and Grandma and Grandpa and poor old dumb Doris and Sam...

(Getting teary-eyed)

And you gotta kinda hand it to 'em, ya' know what I mean...they kept on doin' it, okay...they kept on gettin' up in the morning, doin' their sad little bullshit lives, and I'm the only one who's left who knows their sad little stories...and after I'm gone their sad little stories will be gone...and I thought it would be nice to share some of their sad little tragic everyday little heartbreaking stories with the people who are coming tomorrow night, because, I'll tell ya', these people have stories too...these people who are coming tomorrow night all have sad little tragic everyday little heartbreaking stories and they're suffering... these people are suffering, and this is from personal observation: The average guy on the street kind of person is suffering, and the average woman on the street kind of person is suffering, and there's an isolation there, okay...there's a fear there...and they'll be coming out of their little houses tomorrow night all scared and apprehensive, reaching out, hoping to connect with other sad, apprehensive, isolated, wounded, suffering people…so they can tell each other their sad little tragic everyday little heartbreaking stories…and I want them to know that they're not alone…I want them to know that it's okay to be scared and isolated, it's *normal* to be scared and isolated, because I'll tell ya', night after night these people are locked up in their little homes tuning in for another episode of fear and chaos and random acts of violence, and they get all worked up about it and pissed off about it and terrified about it, and then they try to go to sleep and forget about it, and all they can hear are the voices screaming inside their head and the *pound, pound, pound, pound, pound of their angry…hungry… lonely…heart.*

(*Long beat as he crosses, picks up the pieces of the chair and carries them downstage center and dumps them over the front of the stage. There's a beat.*)

I'm feeling a lot better now. Everything's been goin' a whole lot better lately, and the thing that turned the whole thing around was figuring out that my bed was supposed to be placed so that it was *facing* the door, but not *directly* facing the door, but sort of *kitty-corner* to the door, because there's a whole system, okay…a whole ancient Chinese system and they have the whole thing figured out, and the position of the children is over here

(*Indicating*)

and the position of knowledge is down here

(*Indicating*)

and the position of health is here in the center

(*Indicating*)

and it's a reassuring kind of thing in an unreassuring kind of world…and it gives the whole thing a sort of a meaning, and I'd been looking for meaning for a long time, and that's what a lot of my poetry was all about, and I couldn't find meaning and so I suffered and then I learned that if ya' get everything in the right place, facing the right way, in the right segment of the room, then the *ch'i* moves around the way it's supposed to move around, then everything else takes care of itself.

(He picks up the phone.)

Hello… Is this Mary Beth? Mary Beth Latimore? …I bet you'll never guess who this is…I bet you'll never guess who this is, because you never knew that I even existed, okay…but I was in love with you…totally completely forevermore in love with you, and I used to cry myself to sleep at night, because I wanted to take you to the Ringling Brothers Barnum and Bailey Circus and you just laughed at me and broke my little heart. Do you know what that means? Do you know what it means to have your little heart broken and lose all hope, and because of you I became a poet…

(Beat)

Sparky Litman…*Sparky Litman*, S-P-A-R…listen, Mary Beth, I was just thinkin', ya' know, that maybe you might like to come on over tomorrow night and join me and some nice, normal, isolated, wounded, suffering friends of mine and the fabulous Miss Tina Turner for a little party sort of thing…just a nice easy-going wine and cheese kind of stand-up thing, because I'm trying to create some nice memories, okay. I never had any nice memories, and there are a lot of other people who've never had any nice memories, and I'm inviting a few of these people over and I thought maybe you'd like to come over too…

(He hangs up the phone.)

I always like to give people a second chance. I want to say that again: I always like to give people a second chance…because you never know what could have happened, maybe it was a misunderstanding…maybe it was a miscommunication, and she was just as scared as I was and as overwhelmed as I was, and she knew I was looking at her and she wanted to look back, but that whole puberty-adolescence-hormone thing was going on and it was embarrassing, ya' know what I mean…and I didn't used to feel that way about giving people a second chance when I was writing poetry… because when you're writing poetry you're only thinking about revenge, okay…and it's all payback time, every line, every stanza, every word is like a perfectly poisoned arrow aimed at somebody's rotten little unforgiving heart, and I was writing some really vicious, hateful, not-at-all-uplifting kind of poetry that had a lot of dirty words, body-part kind of words, and I was sending it to people, signed and inscribed… And then last night all of a sudden I couldn't do it any more. Something snapped. It just snapped. And I was sitting there writing this really poisonous, foul, nasty, take-no-prisoners kind of verbal swill, and I just stopped. Just stopped. And there weren't any more words, okay, no more words, not a single word, not a single thought, no hate, no anger, no remorse, no nothin'…and I put down my pencil and realized that I'd never write another word again. Not a word. Again. Ever.

(Beat)

And for the first time in my life…I felt like I was free.

(He looks down, sees an ant, and quietly steps on it.)

(Blackout)

END OF PLAY

www.ingramcontent.com/pod-product-compliance
Lightning Source LLC
Chambersburg PA
CBHW070108100426
42743CB00012B/2691